Fitness Foundry

How to Become an A-List Personal Trainer

I0026774

FUNDAMENTALS FOR OPTIMAL SERVICE-BRANDING-SUCCESS

JULIO A. SALADO NSCA-RCPT*D

Fitnessfoundry.net

Copyright © 2018 Julio A. Salado

All rights reserved. No part of this book may be used or reproduced by any means, graphic, electronic, or mechanical, including photocopying, recording, taping or by any information storage retrieval system without the written permission of the publisher, except in the case of brief quotations embodied in critical articles and reviews.

ISBN: 978-0-9993203-2-7

CONTENTS

山

"I've learned that people will forget
what you said, people will forget what
you did, but people will never forget
how you made them feel."

—MAYA ANGELOU

INTRODUCTION

My book will help anyone considering a career in fitness to understand the principles of becoming an A-List full time personal trainer. I will provide insights on what I call "The Dark Side of Personal Training." This information is not included in any certification program nor is it covered in the mainstream media.

You will learn practical, real world methods and tips that you can apply today. Club owners and fitness managers can also use this book as a checklist for their staff to bring their team to A-List status!

I will also explain what questions to ask in an interview, how many hours you should expect to train, what to expect the first 90 days of employment, and what it takes to have a full client base.

Your first question may be: What is an A-List personal trainer? Regardless of your experience and physical appearance (you do not have to look like a fitness model), an A-List trainer consistently exemplifies specific skills and attributes of past or current successful personal trainers, business leaders, and legendary coaches.

In the following chapters I will outline how to be the best you can be, wherever you are in the process.

> "A huge thank you for everything you have done to help me. You were a great mentor and I really learned a lot especially not having any sales experience. You helped me as a coach, grow my business, and I really do have the utmost respect for you because of one main reason. *You walk the walk and grind every day.* That's how I realized you are the real deal."
>
> —Coach Jack Baldwin, B.S., CSCS

山

"*The secret of getting ahead is getting started. The secret of getting started is breaking your complex overwhelming tasks into small manageable tasks and starting on the first one.*"

—MARK TWAIN

THE DARK SIDE OF PERSONAL TRAINING
Commission Based Sales

The Dark Side begins . . .

There are two facts about commission based personal training. One is that it is a service (not a product) and second is that you have to sell the service. The five-letter word that that you probably do not want to hear is S A L E S! Sales is one part of "The Dark Side of Personal Training" that is often minimized when you consider a personal training career.

In this book, I will focus solely on commission based personal trainers. *Commission* is the key word. The job requires <u>sales</u> to provide the service. Knowing some of the most common challenges and expectations you may encounter before being employed as a personal trainer (certified or not) may assist you in preparing for your new endeavor.

Does the idea of selling make you uncomfortable? No fear, there is always a learning curve in becoming a *professional* salesperson in the fitness industry while building a clientele base. My book will provide you with practical tips and simple strategies to set you up for success. By the way, there is a reason why I added the adjective *professional* in front of salesperson. I'll explain shortly.

Although fitness clubs will invest time and money into helping you develop the skills of a *professional* personal trainer, the first area where they need you to show results is in sales. A few attributes shared by professional salespeople are their interactions with members, communication, body language, careful assessment of the individual's needs and wants, following up, and the ability to show value for their service. While abilities to address each attribute may vary, practicing them is important. These skills are transferable to other industries, which will increase your value as professional. *Note, I'm not mentioning education or fitness experience because you can be hired without either.*

There is a notable distinction between a *professional* salesperson and someone who just mentions price and not value. Becoming a professional salesperson requires a variety of skill sets that can be developed with education, structure, and guidance from a mentor or management.

Anyone who says sales is simple and a small part of the job is misrepresenting the importance of sales for commission-based trainers.

My only suggestion is just to embrace the opportunity to become a *professional* salesperson for a service you know will improve the quality of people's lives. You will be selling the idea to the prospect that their goals are achievable and the bridge between their efforts and tangible results (weight loss or overall fitness) is your customized fitness program and professional guidance.

It's a tough task to sell an idea, yet here is where your passion to be a service provider and succeed at sales intersect.

In a nutshell, you will be developing two distinct skill sets when you enter the personal training industry, namely sales and exercise program design.

It is possible to have monetary success as trainer due to your exceptional ability to sell your services, even though you lack skills in program design. In this scenario, clients are not seeing tangible results, yet you have a full client base. The opposite is more frequent than not, where a trainer is well versed in program design that would bring tangible results but underestimates the challenges in selling their service.

The bottom line is that commission based personal trainers need to build their business usually within a specific time frame of eight months to a year.

> ### *A-List Pro Tip: Engaging with Members*
>
> As commission based trainers we are expected to engage with fitness club members and this will likely feel awkward at first. Just remember that your intention as a service provider is to educate and be helpful. As you engage more with members you will become more comfortable and realize it's our job to approach them. Engaging will also enhance the member experience. Learn to get comfortable with being uncomfortable as this will open new opportunities for building your business.

Prior to employment, the club outlines how management will set weekly and monthly benchmarks to ensure you are trending toward achieving the required sessions to remain a full-time personal trainer.

Unfortunately, even if you have the best personality, multiple degrees or certifications, without achieving the club's minimum requirement for sales during the agreed timeframe, you may be terminated or asked to switch to another department (such as group exercise instructor or member services) if you do not produce.

Commission based employment is not for everyone, and there are clubs that offer a salary. At these facilities, you may find a fulfilling personal trainer experience without the challenges of maintaining a business.

Another underreported fact in building any business is that in the first few months you may see little monetary return in proportion to the amount of time invested in prospecting and hours spent in the gym.

For example, in your first few weeks at the club, you are introducing yourself to members, shadowing veteran trainers, and performing daily responsibilities of maintaining the club's appearance. You will also be participating in the club's training program and providing new members with complimentary sessions.

All along you are being paid a floor rate, which is significantly less than providing personal trainer service. Note, not all gyms offer a flat hourly floor rate. For these clubs that do not offer hourly floor rates, you are not expected to do any duties other than prospect for clients.

Financial planning a safety net to pay your bills is crucial in the first few months. I suggest having six to eight months' worth of savings prior to entering the fitness industry.

There are many benefits to working for a club that provides a floor rate and for those that do not.

If you prepare with savings and understand the challenges that come with being a professional salesperson, then you will be taking a calculated risk.

It is in your best interest to take calculated risks to better your life and personal wealth than go into debt due to underestimating the extent of time it will take to achieve the expected personal training compensation rate/income.

In the next several chapters, I'll get into more details on floor rates, scheduling, and clubs' expectations for the first few months. After reading, you will be well equipped with proven methods for building a personal training business.

> "Julio was an exceptional sales leader and mentor on my team. His pragmatic approach, willingness to share his own expertise and wisdom while listening closely, are all qualities that others around him learned from. Beyond that, as a mentor Julio has always tried to help others become a better version of themselves rather than trying to mold them to his own perspective. His constant support of other team members was invaluable."
>
> Chris Rule, M.B.A., Adjunct Professor of Sports Marketing at Bunker Hill Community College

山

"It is not the strongest of the species that survives, nor the most intelligent that survives. It is the one that is most adaptable to change."

—Charles Darwin

DOUBLE WINNER
Professional Salesperson and Service Provider

You passed your personal training certification exam and are excited to embark on a career that helps people through fitness. You also applied for a commission based personal trainer position and learned about potential income.

The above is my definition of a "double winner." As a professional salesperson, your potential income is based on sales and various bonuses. Secondly, you will have the opportunity to train with people and be a service provider.

There are pros and cons to commission versus salary. In a nutshell, commission-based service providers do not have clients without making sales.

On the flip side, there are salary-based trainers who receive financial security in exchange for a much lower income.

Also, there are some clubs that have a hybrid of commission and salary.

A-List Pro Tip: Appearance and Member Perception

Be mindful that members are observing how you engage and maintain the fitness floor. For example, they do notice if you are walking past an area that is messy, if you are constantly on your phone, or if you are standing with your arms crossed. The first example shows a disinterest in the cleanliness of the club and the latter makes you unapproachable for basics questions. All these actions will reflect on the club's mission, negatively impact the member experience, and decrease opportunities to acquire new leads.

On a side note, education, experience, and skill sets are factors in compensation packages. For example, you may receive a higher hourly split rate because of your experience, specialty certifications, and proven history of sales and/or client results.

If you are commission based, you will be expected to sell your service before you begin training. It does not matter how much experience you do or do not have. Selling is the first step.

Worth noting, you may also enter the industry *without* a personal training certification or experience.

There are many clubs that will hire you based on your intention of getting certified within a specific time frame, along with meeting club's qualifications. Your compensation package should change upon passing the exam.

Whether you are certified or not, hopefully after reading about the connection between your compensation package and providing the actual service, you'll have a better understanding of how to prepare financially and how to plan for the new career. Lastly, the main driver in becoming a "double winner" is to work diligently on your personal and professional development when no one is watching. This is a hallmark of an A-List Personal Trainer!

"Julio's guidance has truly been the foundation of my personal training business. Coming out of school, I felt as if I had all the tools to be a successful personal trainer. Soon, I realized that there was much more to personal training than exercise prescription and keeping up with the science of fitness. Julio mentored me with sales techniques and the importance of building a strong network through client relationships and trust. He taught me how to treat personal training as a business."

Kyle McGlone, B.S., ACSM C.P.T.

山

"The difference between a success-ful person and others is not a lack of strength, not a lack of knowledge, but rather a lack of will."

—Vince Lombardi

WHAT YOU EXPECT FROM BECOMING A PERSONAL TRAINER VS. REALITY

Why do you want to become a personal trainer?

Helping others through fitness is the answer you will get from 99% of individuals before they get certified as personal trainer.

What do you expect from becoming a personal trainer is more telling. A good exercise is to list your *want*s and *expectations*. These may range from monetary goals to control of your own schedule. You can then compare those to the challenges of building a client base in the first year of employment.

You may be better prepared for disappointment when your "wants" are not satisfied in your expected timeframe.

By having an awareness of what to expect and the timeline, you will better be equipped and prepared to build a business.

List your expectations:

- Do you want to be part time or full time?

- Do you want to have your own brand?

- How many clients would you like to train in the first 45 days?

- How many hours per week are you willing to work to obtain your goal?

- What hours in the day do you *not* want to work?

- Would you work on the weekends? If not, list reasons.

- How much monthly income do you need to maintain food and shelter?

- List two to three daily or weekly conveniences you are willing to give up. Examples include personal workouts, going to the movies, eating out.

- How much do you expect to make the first year?

- Do you have interest in other specialty certifications e.g. spin, group exercise, yoga?

- Have you saved six to eight months' of living expenses, including covering credit card debt?

- Do you have support from family and friends?

As a commission-based employee, your pay will be contingent on how many hours of service you provide. I'm going to exclude monthly, quarterly, and other incentives gyms may have when either you or the personal training team hits a quota.

Also, it is important to remember your split for the hourly rate may be low in the beginning due to your experience or club's compensation program for new employees.

Secondly, unless you are bringing in a full client base to the club (which is very rare) then you should expect to take a pay cut for the first few months until your business begins to grow.

A-List Pro Tip: Daily Basis Drill

Sales is repetition of daily actions and administrative work. Create small daily goals based on your weekly and monthly sales goals. It can be to get three new names, schedule one new appointment, or follow up from a conversation. Even if you are successful with your daily goal, it's important to continue the practice to grow and maintain your business. This requires some self-motivation, and expect that you will not be inspired every day. Regardless, make the effort to keep the practice fresh.

Again, to lessen the financial impact on your living expenses and lifestyle, I highly suggest having savings for six to eight months.

I choose this timeframe because by the end of eight months, regardless of whether you have a full client base, you will have a better idea if you want to continue on as a commission based personal trainer or salesperson.

By the way, some clubs expect month-to-month signs of business growth. If your sales numbers do not meet their sales projections, they may decide to offer you another position or terminate employment.

Being a salesperson is not for everyone, and fortunately there are clubs that offer salary-based employment.

The main take-away for commission based personal training is if you leave a club because of low sales, you now have a sales history and can learn from experience and build from it at another club.

It is very common for personal trainers to have low sales due to inexperience or underestimating the connection between sales and providing a service.

Be sure to make notes of your experience at the club and your interactions with all levels of management and departments.

Note how they market themes and seasonal campaigns at the club or online. This is a valuable lesson in how to prospect.

Based on your experience, you should also keep a list of what "not to do" at a club. This may range from witnessing poor customer service to the importance of gym cleanliness.

In the right club environment, you will build your business at a faster pace than at the previous club.

山

"Starting your own business isn't just a job—it's a way of life."

—RICHARD BRANSON

WHAT YOUR CLUB EXPECTS FROM YOU AND HOW IT AFFECTS YOUR EXPECTATIONS

The club you choose to work for understands that it's mutually beneficial for you to be a successful commissioned personal trainer. The club benefits both from your service and your presence on the fitness floor.

It is well documented that members will be less likely to cancel their membership when they are engaged in other services, e.g. personal training or group exercise classes.

Unlike a group exercise class, where there is no fee for the members, fee based personal training is an extra perk for the club because the club receives a split of the training cost, which helps to keep the doors open. Both are geared for member retention, but only one contributes directly to the bottom line.

In this chapter, I will outline some common fitness club expectations for new commission based personal trainers. I am providing this information, so you can take note on how the club's expectations (ranging from scheduling to actual pay in the first few months) compares to your initial hopes for becoming a personal trainer. *Review your checklist from chapter 4.*

The turnover rate for commission based personal trainers in the first six to eight months is relatively high in compared to the percentage that remains after a year in the same club.

I believe the reason for this is a combination of the following:

- Beginning trainers frequently do not understand or minimize the challenges of selling their service.

- Many clubs overlook valuable tools for building a business such as assignment of a mentor or veteran trainer to a new trainer.

- Early poor conversion rates may discourage trainers from learning from their mistakes and improving sales performance.

- Trainers are not always interested in doing duties other than personal training.

It's good to remember, the club is investing in you with the expectation of a monetary return. The hiring process and education offered (though not all clubs offer education) takes time and costs money.

A-List Pro Tip: Non-Physical Activities

Consider the practice of meditation (sitting or Tai Chi), yoga, or activities that allow your mind to unplug and reset mind and body. Many new trainers underestimate the mental and physical toll that can result from the pressure of meeting personal sales goals, especially if they are new to selling. Using daily readings to center your thoughts may better prepare you for the day ahead. Be creative, and make time for yourself each day.

As mentioned before, fee based personal training is extra (ancillary) revenue that supplements the main revenue from new members and contributes to member retention, which keeps the lights on and doors open gym.

With that being said, as a commissioned-based trainer, your duties and the expectations of you at a club will be two-fold. You will be expected to provide an excellent membership experience and create revenue from personal training.

Here are a few examples of additional duties you may be asked to perform:

- Giving tours to new members.

- Participating in member contests/challenges that promote your services.

- Attending outside membership recruitment events at local businesses.

- Leading free small group exercise workshops.

Compensation may not be provided as the club is offering a marketing opportunity that may lead to new prospects for your personal training business.

As you begin your training career at a club, you will likely be working floor shifts and earning an hourly floor rate. Note, not all clubs offer floor shifts, but we will assume they do in this section.

What is an hourly floor rate?

The floor rate is a based on hourly compensation for providing specific duties while building your personal training business.

It is often minimum wage.

For a floor shift you will be given a set schedule where you may have to open or close the club. Sometimes you may do both! We call this "cloping." Closing the club on Monday night and opening the club bright and early on Tuesday.

The main take away is always to inquire about club's expectations from you for the first few months.

By doing this you, will be able to make an informed decision about working for the club or adjust your financial and personal expectations for employment.

There are many benefits to working for a club that provides an hourly floor rate.

"Julio has been a mentor in our company for over three years and has had incredible success with assisting our team of personal trainers to understand the value of being an effective salesperson as it relates to building a successful training business. He has shown incredible prowess in terms of mentoring for sales and professional development with all types of personalities, skill sets, and levels of experience."

Lindsey Cambridge, B.A., Fitness Director

山

"If you align expectations with reality,
you will never be disappointed."
—Terrell Owens

BENEFITS OF PARTNERING WITH A LOCAL CLUB
From Finances to Education

L ocation, location, location! One of the most common factors for success in brick and mortar business is location.

As discussed before, one of the benefits of working at a club versus training independently is the access to members.

When choosing a club, take note of its location's proximity to businesses, residences, future business, and housing development, public transportation and even local competition.

By doing your homework on the location, you are thinking like an entrepreneur. You are essentially a small business and want to choose a location that increases your chances of financial success along with professional development.

It's 100% possible to have a successful online personal training business; however, for our purpose we will discuss providing our service in person or face to face. Remember, I am covering topics for commission based personal trainers that require sales to render services.

Later in the book in chapter 7, "Creating Your Personal Brand Prior to Being Hired", I discuss the benefits of having a hybrid business of online services and training at a club.

I do make the disclaimer to adhere to your employer's policies. By doing so, it allows you to develop your brand and to solicit prospects for the club, so it is mutually beneficial. All of this can be done while preventing any conflict of interest between the two parties.

But first, let's get to know the difference between different types of gyms, along with their general expectations about employment. Hopefully, this information may assist you in choosing where to start your career.

The major benefits from working at a corporate gym, studio, nonprofit wellness center, or local club.

Overhead Costs

You do not have to worry about paying rent, but you are expected to provide revenue that contributes to the overall financial needs of the club.

Other than exclusive personal training boutiques, most clubs' main source of revenue comes from membership. Personal training is considered ancillary revenue and your main role would be to build your business and split your sales with the gym. Leave the daily operations to management and focus on becoming a part of a team.

Sales Leads/Prospect Pool

A big advantage of working in a gym as a commission based personal trainer is access to members. More members equal more opportunities to educate them on how your services may be the bridge to their fitness goals.

Also, it's well known in the fitness industry that there is a higher conversion of prospects to members when they interact positively with the personal trainer team and other club employees.

Make a point to work with membership during their tours; even saying hello to a prospect can create a lasting impression.

Your friendliness may be the reason why someone joins the club!

A-List Pro Tip: Ask About Their Goals

When engaging with a member on the fitness floor be sure to ask what their goals are and what their plan for the day is. It is a sincere question and will start conversation that can be used to inform the member of your services, an opportunity to provide tips, and most importantly it shows you support their goals.

Most clubs will have a membership team or individual whose main role is soliciting, marketing, giving tours, and converting prospects to members. Getting an individual to come to the club is a tough task in itself. This is then followed by a process of showing how the gym membership is the best value in the area. Membership enrollment is not solely based on equipment, rather it's a combination of classes, services, amenities, and the overall environment on which decisions are based.

Fortunately, you do not have to worry about membership sales and getting access to new leads! Membership will provide that pipeline of prospects; however, it is important to note that dependence on membership for new leads is not conducive to building a long-term business.

With assistance from management and willingness to learn, you will develop specific sales and communication skills to generate your own leads. It's my experience that building relationships with members is the foundation for creating opportunities for converting members to clients.

On a side note, new leads for your business are usually distributed by management or membership. It's a common practice to offer a complimentary appointment with a trainer as part of a new membership package. The numbers of complimentary appointments and the name of the service may vary.

There are two main objectives for the complimentary appointment. One is to provide an excellent membership experience. Two is to show how personal training services will optimize the prospect's efforts and help them achieve their fitness goals.

If you have a consistent record of no conversions, by which I mean meeting for a complimentary personal training session but not converting them into clients, then you may temporarily not get as many (or any) NEW member leads!

This is a one of the "Dark Sides" of personal training as a commissioned employee that is rarely discussed.

Some clubs (such as nonprofits) may not emphasize sales in contrast to privately owned gyms or those publicly traded on the stock market. In either scenario, if you are a commission-based employee, it's up to you to be proactive with membership and the club's member base.

In a nutshell, your chances of building clientele as a commission-based service provider is significantly higher working under the umbrella of a club. Secondly, you will be exposed to and may have the opportunity to learn the management side of maintaining and growing a club.

Another benefit of working at a club, especially in your first year, is education through exposure to other trainers with various experience and skill sets.

As an entrepreneur, always work to grow your network by seeking out professionals with established success. Starting your career with a club is a stepping stone to achieving longevity and financial fulfillment in the industry.

山

*"Find a group of people who challenge
and inspire you, spend a lot of time with
them, and it will change your life."*

—Amy Poehler

CREATE YOUR PERSONAL BRAND PRIOR TO BEING HIRED

What's in a name or brand? Everything! The brand reflects your services, mission, and core values. Your brand will also evolve as you grow with experience both professionally and personally. It's meaning will deepen as time goes on, and you may even change the name to reflect your personal growth.

Regardless, by developing your own brand your ability to present and passionately communicate your service becomes easier and more personal. The main objective is to convert prospects to clients. You want to them to believe in your service and invest in personal training.

With a personal brand and an online presence, you can showcase your skills with videos, blogs, posts to social media, etc.

I call having your own website "virtual real estate." It's irrelevant how flashy it is in the beginning. The first step is to buy the domain name and then build from there. It can be a simple landing page with your picture, services offered, and contact info.

Think of it as a business card. The cost is minimal. With time you will learn more about how to use it as tool for monetization. Consider using the same brand name across other social media platforms. It's also okay to have more than one brand name.

Important: Let's be clear about conflicts of interest when working for an employer. It's very important for you to read their policies and non-compete agreement carefully.

A-List Pro Tip: Offering to Meet One on One

This is a follow up from my other A-List Pro Tip of asking a potential client about their goals. There is a process in building a relationship with members, and the first step is to introduce yourself and to find out the member's goals. After this is established, it's important after the first contact to offer a meeting with you and briefly explain how it would benefit them. The practice of offering to meet will help develop your communication skills plus spark new conversation. If they decline you can still offer to be a resource if you learn about new equipment or exercises that may help them with their goals. Regardless, always be courteous and learn what you could do better at the next opportunity.

The purpose of your own brand is to solicit followers and solicit new sales. The prospects for personal training can then be directed to your current place of employment.

The purpose of the exercise below is to get you started. It can be used as a template. You do not have to reinvent the wheel when contemplating your brand. Be creative and have fun.

Here are few suggestions to get you started on creating your own brand.

You will need a pen and paper to take notes.

- List two to five fitness professionals you currently follow, subscribe to, or wish to emulate.

- Note their brand name and/or trademark and see if it mirrors what they deliver as content or service.

- Review the font style, color, number of words, and write down why it's marketable.

Now here's a tough but fun exercise . . .

- Your brand reflects you! Think of the events that lead to your decision to become a personal trainer.

- Were there any sports you played that changed your life?

- Did you overcome or manage any mental or physical health issues or injuries with exercises? For example, losing weight because you were at risk for high blood pressure.

- Were you positively impacted by a coach and since then you wanted to help others?

- Has physical exercise helped manage both your mental and physical health?

Now imagine you have an opportunity to open up a studio directly across the street from an established gym or a location lacking a fitness club.

- What would the name be? The name or phrase should reflect a combination of your experience that was the basis for you becoming a personal trainer. Here are few examples from trainers I mentored e.g. Revival Fitness, Paradigm Studio, Renaissance Fitness, Better You Health Club

- Be sensitive to the demographics you are intending to service. For example, if the area is in a business district with mostly sedentary individuals then you probably do not want a specialty brand or modality of fitness that will limit your prospects.

On a side note, I would strongly suggest checking if the name is available as a domain or being used on social media. If not, purchasing a domain is very inexpensive and you can think of it as virtual real estate. You can always work on it in the future.

Registering your brand on social media gives you access to a broader audience and is an excellent tool to market your services and build a professional network.

Once you think of the name, then you can create an image that represents your personality and service. The image is optional, but it can be fun and is useful for marketing. You will then explain how it symbolizes your brand of fitness. The symbol does not have to be related to fitness.

It's important to create a brand that targets the demographic in the area, so you can attract more business. I need to stress what is most important is your ability to EXPLAIN why you chose the name! It's a process in refining the skill of presentation and you will get better with practice.

- Keep the explanation short and simple on what the brand/ name symbolizes and how it connects to the prospective client's goals.

At this point, without mentioning your brand, you can now talk to prospects at the club with more confidence regarding your services.

This is a win-win scenario. You bring in new prospects for membership to your employer's club and *you* gain a client! This is all done while respecting the club's policies.

This action would speak volumes of your entrepreneurial mindset to your employer and most importantly prevents your client base from being solely dependent on internal membership sales.

Time is of the essence as a commission-based trainer. As discussed, you cannot provide your services without sales. Therefore, I suggest beginning the process of creating your own brand prior to being employed at a club.

山

"Whatever you can do, or dream you can, begin it. Boldness has genius, power, and magic in it."

—Goethe

YOU ARE HIRED! NOW WHAT ABOUT THOSE SALES?

B y now, you understand the theme of my book is to inform you of what's expected as a commission based personal trainer. I now want to give you some insights, so you can be best equipped to become an A-List Personal Trainer.

Learning how to sell your service is a process. You will find that the word *sales* may be called *value* by your employer. Regardless of the term, at the end of the day, commission-based trainers cannot render their services without making sales. Simply stated, you need to convert a prospect into a paying client. This completes the sales process.

Ironically, you can have little to no experience as a certified personal trainer and still excel in sales. The skill these individuals possess is the ability to motivate or make their prospect feel and believe the personal training service is a worthy investment.

Later, I will discuss the most underused and overlooked skill in selling personal training, that is being a "motivator."

Here is the crux of why it is difficult to sell personal training. You need to convince a prospect what is best for them with regard to achieving their fitness goals.

A-List Pro Tip: Task or To-Do List

Your daily actions of seeking out leads along with follow ups can be overwhelming unless you are using a to-do list. There are many free apps that allow you to create different tasks that can be very useful in reminding you of daily or weekly goals and important follow ups. For example, you may meet someone on the floor today and you were able to get their name and goals. You would then enter this into your to-do list and have it handy for the next time you see them, with the next goal being to get an appointment or provide a tip for their goals. Developing relationships is fundamental for building a business.

In a short period of time, usually in a consultation session, you try to build a relationship of trust with the prospect and ask them to make an investment with no guarantees. They are not buying a product; they are buying into your vision of them achieving their goals.

To recap, at the core of the prospect's decision to invest is how they feel. Are they motivated to make a change now?

Remember as discussed earlier, the club will split your personal training rate and the revenue you generate is factored into the club's expenses.

Why do sales matter for staying employed with a club?

One reason is the following: If you are given health benefits as a commission based personal trainer, and after a few months you are not meeting the club's established minimum of paid employee hours, the benefits you receive become a loss for the club.

Secondly, there is the club's projected personal training revenue from the previous year. Your assigned personal sales goals will be derived from the overall team monthly sales quota.

Please note, clubs may also decide to terminate you or offer you another position based on your sales performance after a period of time. The club's expectations and requirements should be in the job description and in the job offer. If not, then protect yourself and ask for written job requirements.

Clubs will usually give a specific amount of time to achieve a number of paid hours or sessions that would qualify you for other benefits such as an increase in split percentage of hourly pay, monthly bonus, etc.

The following is a basic outline for the first few weeks and months at a club as a commission based personal trainer. This may vary depending on whether or not you are certified. If certified, you will be expected to sell. If you are not certified, you will be allotted time to pass the certification course.

Honeymoon Period. Weeks 1–4:

- You understand the minimum paid hours required to stay employed and/or receive health benefits.

- You may be required to attend in-house professional development workshops, e.g. sales, club's fitness assessment protocols, etc.

- You will learn basic duties other than personal training, e.g. cleaning equipment.

- You may be required to shadow trainers as they train clients.

- You will learn safety procedures.

- Your manager will assign daily and weekly goals other than sales, e.g. getting names of members.

- Your manager will set your monthly sales goal.

- You will have opportunities to practice selling your services.

- You will begin to offer your services to members.

Post Honeymoon Period. Week 5–10:

- Expectations have been set for monthly sales goal and you understand the consequences if these are not achieved.

- You may have weekly meetings with management on your

sales progress and performance.

- You will still be required to continue with all duties related to your employment.

- Based on your sales, you should assess if you are meeting your financial needs.

After ten weeks you will know if it's in your best interest to continue and if the job meets your financial and personal expectations.

If you are struggling with sales, remember that it does not reflect your passion or fitness level or expertise. You may grow your client base faster in another club due to your recent experience. Also, you may choose to become a salary-based trainer rather than commission base.

The main take away is do not give up on your dream! Your experience is a stepping stone.

山

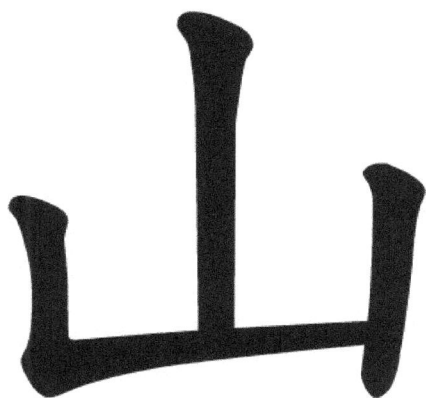

"*It's what* you learn after *you know* it all that counts."

—JOHN WOODEN

HOW TO BECOME
AN A-LIST PERSONAL
TRAINER

Regardless of your physical appearance (as I stated earlier, you do not need to look like a fitness model), experience in the fitness industry, or your particular skill sets, you now have the tools to become an A-List Personal Trainer.

You don't need to take a special course or get certification, either!

The formula I'll outline below is simple but not easy. It will take some daily practice, and best of all, there's no pass or fail.

Your success is based on walking through feelings of being uncomfortable and learning from each experience.

Here are a few points:

Becoming an A-List Personal Trainer starts with your decision to go above and beyond in providing exceptional customer service to everyone you come in contact with professionally, not just your clients.

Underlining principles and practices:

- Helping others without expectations or conditions is key.

- The more people you connect and build a relationship with, the bigger your pool of qualified prospects becomes.

- Low cost, big returns . . . the biggest investment is the time you spend with members.

Believe you can improve the quality of people's lives:

- Base this belief on your own experience. Think of a time you overcame personal challenges through exercise or interaction with a coach who made an impact on your development.

- Communicate your experience and connect it to the member's goals. This helps to build a relationship of trust and can inspire them to use your service.

- At the very least, you have motivated someone to continue. They will remember this.

Pair your passion and experience with your education:

- As a certified personal trainer, you are qualified to develop programs that help others achieve their fitness goals.

- You will use exercise science as the foundation of personalized programs.

- You'll refer clients out when their needs are beyond your current skill set (in the industry it's called "staying within scope of your knowledge").

Understand the power of coaching and how it impacts people's lives:

- Personal training is about more than physical activity; there are many ways to help others build strength and confidence. You are a source of inspiration.

- Making people feel good about themselves is priceless.

- Strive to be known as the friendliest employee in the club. You never know when you'll have the opportunity to help someone unless you are approachable.

The next step is to reach even more individuals. The Internet is the best platform for seeking a wider audience.

- As we discussed earlier, your online brand is now a health and fitness resource along with your other services, e.g. personal training, nutrition counseling.

- Take advantage of social media marketing campaigns and have fun in providing health and fitness information.

- Make a small investment in branded merchandise such as apparel and accessories.

Network with fitness professionals locally and online:

- This may lead to new opportunities ranging from education, marketing, and even future employment.

- You can also use it to seek mentors and coaches for your areas of improvement such as sales, fitness assessment.

- Interview your favorite coach or ask local business leaders what their best practices are. This can be from any industry.

There is no board that concludes if you are an A-List Personal Trainer, so how will you know you've arrived?

You will have unexpected positive comments and recognition in how you exemplify excellent customer service, reliability, and professionalism.

Successful personal trainers, business leaders, and legendary coaches all share similar attributes, regardless of their specialty or industry.

Two of the most common skills are listening to the needs of the client, followed by repeatedly referring to the solution to their needs. We help others believe their goal is achievable, and we are the bridge to their success.

We also learn from each appointment, regardless of whether or not we closed a sale. It's extremely important to identify areas for personal improvement. This requires an honest appraisal of the day's work and the willingness to make changes.

Lastly, practice daily self-care for both mind and body. Going beyond physical activity, seek connection with your network of support. This will fuel your passion to deliver exceptional service. It will also create opportunities to reach more people in the day.

Earlier in the book, I described the dark side of personal training as a commissioned employee, and now I have outlined the "bright side" of personal training, that is, fulfilling your desire to help others through health and fitness while achieving financial success.

By simply practicing these principles each day to the best of your ability, you will earn the title of "A-List Personal Trainer."

Learn more about my educational programming and CEU approved workshops for building, marketing, and retaining a full clientele business.

- PT Sales 101: The What, When and How to Sell Personal Training!

- "BREAK OUT of Breaking Even!" 3 Step Methods for Proven Long-Term Weight Loss

- How to Become an A-List Personal Trainer!

For a full list of courses designed for fitness managers, gym owners, and personal trainers contact me at juliosalado@ fitnessfoundry.net or visit www.fitnessfoundry.net

山

"Strategy without tactics is the slowest route to victory. Tactics without strategy is the noise before defeat."

— SUN TZU

A-LIST PERSONAL TRAINING TIPS AND STRATEGIES

The following thoughts are pulled from my continuing education workshops. These include basic strategies to assist in prospecting, how to use technology for marketing, and tips for personal growth and professional development.

From my personal experience and years of mentoring, I have identified some of the best methods that are practical and effective for building a business.

The greatest investment will be your time — the time you take to build your brand and relationships.

My hope is that these three suggestions will help you as they have helped countless other personal trainers who rely on sales to provide their services.

"In my 14 years in the fitness industry I have seen that there is often a gap between the technical knowledge that a personal trainer possesses and the ability to articulate and engage that information to a potential client. Julio Salado truly understands how to bridge that gap and how to paint a simple picture so that all type of personal trainers can understand the importance. After one seminar our team came away with some immediate simple strategies to add to their approach, which lead to a direct improvement in engagement with our membership base."

—Tim Botto, Director of Operations
WANG YMCA OF CHINATOWN,
YMCA OF GREATER BOSTON

Education

We educate members, clients, and prospects throughout our interactions with them.

Second to educating is repetition of the basics because it's my job to help them understand how and why they are making progress toward their goals (or why they are not making progress).

In regard to prospects, I begin to build a relationship that shows value through sharing my expertise. I'm a big promoter of "self-efficacy" with my clients, too, helping them help themselves.

Lastly, how I communicate is also important, and the words I use will vary due to an individual's interests and/or personality. You need to become perceptive about people.

Bottom line, I always remind them that I can be one of their resources for health and fitness information. There is a ton of misinformation in the media, and I want to help them make better decisions about their training, their fitness routine, and their weight loss goals if they have any. You are their conduit to overall fitness and good health.

Regardless of whether you are just starting to build your business or have a full client base, offering to be a resource can help with client retention, growth, and referrals.

We want to promote conversation and questions so we can show our value as personal trainers.

Building a business starts by building relationships with prospective clients and maintaining communication with new clients as well as those who have stopped their training.

Learn How to Create and Finesse Those Always Useful Group Email Lists!

Email is another platform to share your health and fitness knowledge while working on your business! You offer up value and they get to benefit from your knowledge. Win-win!

Here are a few types of groups email lists you can consider to help your networking.

A. "Prospect Follow Up" List:

If you offer advice to a member while on the fitness floor, politely ask if you can keep in touch via email and follow up with other tips and/or invite them for a complimentary session.

The point is, you don't want to keep them from their workout, and by offering to send an email you'll have a chance to follow up with them.

B. "Decline Personal Training" List:

Members who you met for complimentary session but declined to buy personal training.

Thank them for meeting with you. Then, ask them if you could periodically reach out and check in on their progress and brief them on new workshops or promotions, or share information related to their goals. Make sure they know you are here for them. Especially when the going gets rough or they are experiencing a fitness plateau from their workout routine.

C. "Inactive Clients" List:

After your client decides to stop training, remind them that you will periodically check in with their progress and share information related to their goals. You can also mention that their referrals are much appreciated. Building a business starts by building relationships.

There's nothing better than real face time or one-on-one conversation with a prospect; however, we usually need to build trust and a relationship prior to getting that appointment.

It's 100% possible to show your sincerity and desire to be of service via email.

We want to promote conversation and questions, so we can show our value as personal trainers.

That is just a few group email examples. If you start today, in three to six months you'll have more.

You will also get better with creating email campaigns and targeting specific demographics and needs, keeping in mind creative ways to approach these communications.

"Work ethic is the most important component of being successful."

—Kliff Kingsbury

Below are two examples of my personal training PRO tips for daily learning and for building good work ethics.

PT PRO Tip: Importance of feedback from peers for professional growth.

I am always searching for the best way to communicate basic principles of exercise with my clientele, members and personal training team. Their feedback keeps me motivated.

Sometimes when I listen to one of my peers, their choice of words is more precise and easier to understand than how I might explain the same exercise or movement principle.

Here's one I want to ask YOU:

How would you explain the following to a client or prospect from the general population? This must be no more than two to three sentences.

What is the difference between "open" and "closed" chain exercises and benefits?

I would explain it with a visual example along with a brief difference between the two. This is what I would say . . . *"A step up to a box is an 'open chain' exercise and a squat is a 'closed chain.' For this 'Open chain' exercise, you would temporarily bring one foot off the floor. This requires balance and you will recruit more stabilizer muscles, unlike when in a squat where both feet remain on the floor. They both should be in your workout."*

With regard to communication, the "less is more" strategy is very useful. The objective is to promote questions and conversation with clients and prospects. I'm an advocate of self-efficacy. My definition of self-efficacy is empowering clients and prospects with tools and education.

PT PRO Team Tip: The value of respecting other trainers' clients!

While on the fitness floor, I recently suggested a member meet with me to discuss her goals and review her current program. As we were scheduling via email, she mentioned she had worked with another trainer at the club. She did not mention this in person.

As I was not aware of this, I promptly referred her back to that trainer. I looped him in and moved on. The member will always have the option to work with me in the future.

It has been my experience to be transparent as soon as possible with other trainers when their clients show an interest in working with me.

I believe having a good work ethic benefits the team, my relationship with other trainers, and the member experience.

Final Thoughts

My best advice on becoming an effective A-List Personal Trainer:

1. Stay within your scope of knowledge at first; then seek to expand your skill set.

2. Always look for areas of improvement especially in how you communicate with others.

3. Be willing to offer support between sessions via telephone, email, and/or text.

4. Find a mentor!

山

"What you get by achieving your goals is not as important as what you become by achieving your goals."

—Henry David Thoreau

RESOURCES, SOCIAL MEDIA AND CONTACT

Fitness Foundry Services:

- Online Weight Loss Programs

- 1:1 Personal Training

- Personal and Group Training

- Elite Training for Sports Professionals

- Post Rehabilitation Training

- Group Instruction for Beginner's Yang Tai Chi Chuan

- Consultation on Personal Training Business Management

- Continue Education Provider Workshops

Also available *"BREAK OUT* of Breaking Even!" 3 Step Method for PROVEN Long-Term Weight Loss. ISBN: 978-0-9993203-0-3

Available in print on Amazon and eBook for Kobo, Kindle, iBook and Nook

Follow me on social media:

Facebook: www.facebook.com/fitnessfoundry also www.facebook.com/a-listpersonaltrainer

Twitter: www.twitter.com/fitnessfoundry

Instagram: www.instagram.com/fitnessfoundryUSA

YouTube: www.youtube.com/user/fitnessfoundry

For CEU Approved Workshops and more information.

Website: www.fitnessfoundry.net

Website: www.a-listpersonaltrainer.com

Email: juliosalado@fitnessfoundry.net

ABOUT THE AUTHOR

Specialties:

Julio Salado- National Strength & Conditioning Assoc. -Recognized Certified Personal Trainer with Distinction., U.S.A.W. Olympic Lifting Coach, U.S.A.P.L. Powerlifting Coach, TRX & Kettle bell Certified Instructor, National Assoc. of Sports Medicine Corrective Exercise Specialist, Certified Pre-Post Natal & Tai Chi Chuan 22 Form Instructor.

Training Philosophy:

My personal training is based on exercise science and holistic arts. I am also a mentor, educator and continuing education provider.

My experience is over 10 years of experience in cross-training with disciplines in bodybuilding, Olympic lifts, post-rehab training, senior fitness, sports performance & Tai Chi Chuan. I have successfully worked with clients 18-92 years of age from different backgrounds, pre-conditions, fitness levels and goals.

I am also the author of "BREAK OUT of Breaking Even!" 3-Step Method for PROVEN Long-Term Weight Loss.

My health & fitness essays and videos have been published in print and online such as **"Boston Mayor Marty Walsh's Senior Count TV Show","Boston.com 'Health and Family Magazine' , "Fitness Professional Online", "Boston Globe , "Boston Magazine"** and "Top Personal Trainers Answer Your Questions" published by Regency Publishing.

No one is exempt from the benefits of living their dreams. Witness the results and experience the benefits of investing in yourself.

Be well and stay ACTIVE!!

Julio A. Salado, NSCA RCPT*D
USAW & USAPL Coach
Fitness Foundry designed for healthy living©.
Founder
Assess, **I**nitiate, **M**otivate
www.fitnessfoundry.net

As seen on…

ALLIANCE
AMBASSADOR

The Boston Globe

Testimonials:

"Julio's guidance has truly been the foundation of my personal training business. Coming out of school, I felt as if I had all the tools to be a successful personal trainer. Soon, I realized that there was much more to personal training than exercise prescription and keeping up with the science of fitness. Julio mentored me with sales techniques and the importance of building a strong network through client relationships and trust. He taught me how to treat personal training as a business. I believe that without Julio's mentorship I would not be where I am today."

—Kyle McGlone B.S., ACSM CPT.

"Julio has been a mentor in our company for over three years and has had incredible success with assisting our team of personal trainers to understand the value of being a effective salesperson as it relates to building a successful training business. He has shown incredible prowess in terms of mentoring for sales and professional development with all types of personalities, skill sets, and levels of experience. He meets multiple times a week with each new team member and covers everything from what they are feeling challenged with, to what their strengths are and how they can capitalize on them. He is always looking for new ways to tie the pieces together for new staff and challenge them in new ways. His individual success in personal training and the sales aspect of his business is unprecedented. He truly 'walks the walk and talks the talk' and his successful business demonstrates that!"

—Lindsey Cambridge B.A., Fitness Director

"Julio was an exceptional sales leader and mentor on my team. His pragmatic approach, willingness to share his own expertise and wisdom while listening closely, are all qualities that others around him learned from. Beyond that, as a mentor Julio has always tried to help others become a better version of themselves rather than trying to mold them to his own perspective. His constant support of other team members was invaluable."

—Chris Rule, M.B.A., Adjunct Professor of Sports Marketing at Bunker Hill Community College

"A huge thank you for everything you have done to help me. You were a great mentor and I really learned a lot especially not having any sales experience. You helped me as a coach, grow my business, and I really do have the utmost respect for you because of one main reason. *You walk the walk and grind every day.* That's how I realized you are the real deal."

—Coach Jack Baldwin, B.S., CSCS

www.ingramcontent.com/pod-product-compliance
Lightning Source LLC
Chambersburg PA
CBHW022341280326
41934CB00006B/736